Why do bears go fishing?

Barbara Taylor

Miles
Kelly

First published in 2011 by Miles Kelly Publishing Ltd
Harding's Barn, Bardfield End Green, Thaxted,
Essex, CM6 3PX, UK

2 4 6 8 10 9 7 5 3 1

Publishing Director Belinda Gallagher
Creative Director Jo Cowan
Editorial Director Rosie McGuire
Editor Sarah Parkin
Volume Designer Rocket Design Ltd
Cover Designer Kayleigh Allen
Image Manager Liberty Newton
Indexer Gill Lee
Production Manager Elizabeth Collins
Reprographics Anthony Cambray,
Stephan Davis, Lorraine King

ISBN 978-1-84810-454-9

Printed in China

British Library Cataloguing-in-Publication Data

A catalogue record for this book is
available from the British Library

ACKNOWLEDGEMENTS
The publishers would like to thank the following
artist who has contributed to this book:
Mike Foster (character cartoons)
All other artwork from the Miles Kelly Artwork Bank

The publishers would like to thank the following
sources for the use of their photographs:
Dreamstime.com 6 giant panda Hungchungchih,
American black bear Hilbell, sun bear Petrmasek,
spectacled bear Starper, polar bear F2, sloth bear Mvshiv,
moon bear Karelgallas; 9 Pakra1k974; 13 Oksanaphoto;
15 Loflo69; 17 Anankkml
iStockphoto.com 4 John Pitcher;
7 Klaas Lingbeek-van Kranen; 26 Michel de Nijs
Naturepl.com 29 Eric Baccega

All other photographs are from:
digitalSTOCK, digitalvision, PhotoDisc

Every effort has been made to acknowledge the
source and copyright holder of each picture.
Miles Kelly Publishing apologises for any unintentional
errors or omissions.

Made with paper from a sustainable forest

www.mileskelly.net
info@mileskelly.net

www.factsforprojects.com

Self-publish your
children's book

buddingpress.co.uk

Contents

what is a bear?

A bear is a mammal. Mammals have warm blood, fur or hair, and they feed their babies on milk. Bears have big heads, short legs and thick fur. Female bears give birth to two or three babies (cubs) at a time.

bear president!

Teddy bears are named after an American president called Teddy Roosevelt. He once refused to shoot a bear. After this, toy bears were called teddies.

Brown bear

Cubs

where do bears live?

Spectacled bears live only in the mountains of South America. Each type of bear has its own favourite place to live, from the icy north to hot rainforests.

Spectacled bear

Pretend
Imagine you are a bear and see how fast you can run on all fours, then race your friends.

HOW fast are bears?

Bears usually move slowly on all fours, but they can run surprisingly fast when they have to. Brown bears can charge at 50 kilometres an hour – much faster than most people!

Are all bears the same?

No – there are eight different kinds of bear! Each kind has different colours and markings. The easiest bears to recognize are the black-and-white giant panda and the white polar bear.

Giant panda

American black bear

Sun bear

Moon bear

Brown bear

Sloth bear

Polar bear

Spectacled bear

when is a panda red?

When it's a red panda! Red pandas are not actually bears. They belong to the raccoon family. When it's cold, red pandas curl their long, furry tails around their bodies to keep warm.

Red panda

It's all in the name!

Some ancient peoples thought it would anger bear spirits to call a bear by its name. They made up different names instead, such as 'Darling Old One' or 'Owner of the Earth'.

which bear is not a bear?

A koala bear! Even though koalas are sometimes called 'koala bears', they are not related to bears. Koalas have pouches. They live in Australia and eat eucalyptus leaves.

Find

Ask your friends what names they have given their teddies. How many different names can you find?

which bears are the biggest?

The biggest bears are the brown bears of Kodiak Island in Alaska, and polar bears. Both of these giant bears can weigh as much as a small car! The Kodiak bear has bigger bones than other types of brown bear.

Kodiak bear

Did people live with giant bears?

Yes – people hunted giant cave bears during the last Ice Age. They carved ornaments from their bones. These giant bears died out about 11,500 years ago.

Tallest bear!

The polar bear is the tallest bear alive today. The biggest one measured so far was 3.6 metres tall – that's twice the height of a tall person!

Draw

Create a height chart for your toy animals. Measure each one and draw lines on the chart.

Brown bear

can bears walk like us?

Yes they can! Bears rear up on two legs to get a good view of what is around them or to scare away enemies. Spectacled bear mothers can even walk along on two legs when they are holding their cubs.

Are bears good at climbing trees?

American black bear cubs

Yes! Bears have strong muscles in their legs and shoulders, which help them to scramble up tree trunks easily. Their long, curved claws give a firm grip on tree trunks and branches.

How long are a bear's claws?

A bear's thick, sharp claws are longer than your fingers! Unlike cats, bears can't pull their claws back into their paws. Bears use their claws for climbing trees, finding food and digging holes (dens) for sleeping or resting.

Sun bear's paw and claws

Poor panda!

Pandas sometimes fall out of trees. Their thick fur helps to cushion their bodies as they land.

Do bears build nests?

Bears don't usually build nests, but moon bears build leafy platforms in trees and sleep there. Spectacled bears also build nests in trees from the branches.

Pretend

Imagine you are a moon bear and build a cosy nest of leaves or cushions.

Do pandas ever stop eating?

Giant panda

Not very often! Giant pandas eat mainly bamboo, which is a type of tall, woody grass. Bamboo does not contain much goodness, so pandas have to spend most of their time eating to get the nutrients they need.

Why do bears go fishing?

Bears find it easy to catch salmon when these big fish swim up rivers. Some bears fish from the riverbanks, but others wade right into the water and scoop up fish with their huge paws.

Grizzly bears

Seal supper!

Polar bears wait beside a seal's breathing hole in the ice. When the seal swims up to the hole for air, one swipe from the bear's giant paw kills the seal straight away.

Swim
When you next go swimming, try jumping out of the water like a salmon and see if someone can catch you!

Which bear has the longest tongue?

The sun bear has the longest tongue – it is up to 25 centimetres long! This is very useful for licking up small bugs and reaching into cracks in trees.

Are sloth bears noisy?

Yes! When sloth bears feed at a termite mound, the noise they make can be heard up to 100 metres away! The bears make a tube with their lips and tongue and suck up lots of the tiny termites very quickly.

Sloth bears

Spectacled bear

Make

Draw a bear face on a paper plate. Cut holes for the eyes and use string to tie your mask on.

HOW good is a bear's sense of smell?

Bears have long noses and an excellent sense of smell. A bear often lifts its head to sniff the air, picking up smelly messages about food, danger or other bears.

Football bear!

Some sports teams, such as the Chicago Bears, are named after bears because they are strong, powerful animals.

Do bears have good eyesight?

Bears have small eyes and rely on their senses of smell and hearing more than their sense of sight. Their eyesight is about the same as a person with good eyesight. Bears can see in colour, which helps them to find fruits and berries.

which bear is a good swimmer?

Polar bears are strong swimmers. Mothers teach their cubs to swim while they are small. These bears use their huge front paws to paddle through the water and their back legs for steering.

Polar bear

Cub

How did moon bears get their name?

Moon bears are named after the white or cream patch of fur on their chests, which is shaped like a crescent moon. These bears live in Asia and are also called Asiatic black bears.

Moon bear

Home alone!

Bears live alone, but they may gather in groups to feed. A group of bears is called a sloth, because people thought bears were slow and lazy, like sloths.

Think

Look at the bears in this book and make up some different names for a group of bears.

Do bears have picnics?

Teddy bears might do, but real bears don't. They eat whatever food is available at different times of year. Most bears eat a wide range of food, from grass, berries and honey to insects, fish, birds and mammals.

where do bears go in winter?

Bears that live in places with cold winters sleep through the winter, because there is little food for them to eat. They sleep inside a den, which may be a hole dug in the ground or a safe, sheltered place such as a cave.

Brown bear

which bear gives birth in a snow cave?

In the middle of winter, female polar bears give birth to their tiny cubs inside a snow cave. The cubs stay there for up to five or six months, feeding on their mother's rich milk and growing big and strong.

count

How many hours do you sleep each night? Work out how many hours you sleep in a week.

Cubs

Polar bear

why do bears feast in autumn?

There is lots of food for bears to eat in autumn, such as berries, nuts, fish and insects. Bears eat as much as they can and become quite fat.

Shrinking bear!

During their winter sleep bears don't eat. They use up the energy stored in their body as fat. Bears may lose up to half their body weight by the end of the winter.

when do cubs open their eyes?

Bear cubs are born with their eyes shut. They don't open their eyes until they are about six weeks old. Spectacled bears have pale fur around their eyes, which makes them look like they are wearing glasses!

story bears!

Bears are included in many famous stories, such as *Goldilocks and the Three Bears*.

Spectacled bear cubs

Do father bears look after their cubs?

No – mother bears bring up the cubs. The cubs drink their mother's milk. She teaches them how to find food and shelter, and how to escape from danger.

American black bear

Cubs

How big are bear cubs?

Bear cubs are very small. Polar bear cubs are no bigger than guinea pigs when they are born!

Discover
Use the Internet to find out how much a giant panda cub weighs when it is born.

Do bears give piggybacks?

Sloth bear mothers do! The cubs ride around on her back until they are about nine months old. She has a special patch of fur for the cubs to hang on to. These piggyback rides keep them safe from enemies, including other bears.

Cubs

Sloth bear

Why do male bears fight?

Male bears fight over food, female bears and places to live. They have sharp teeth and claws, and can give each other serious injuries. Most of the time bears keep away from each other to avoid fights.

Brown bears

No winners!

Bears sometimes fight Siberian tigers. They are both strong and the same size, so it is difficult for either to win!

Which bears fought for the Romans?

Atlas bears were captured by the Romans and made to fight people called gladiators. These fierce fights were arranged to entertain people, but were very cruel to the bears.

Draw

Look at pictures of Roman soldiers in books and draw your teddy bear wearing armour.

Which bear loves honey?

Sun bear

All of them do! Sun bears love honey so much they are sometimes called honey bears. They tear open bees' nests with their long claws and lick up the honey. Sun bears are only the size of big dogs, so they can easily climb trees to find nests.

Remember
Can you remember the names of the eight different kinds of bear?

which bear is grizzly?

The brown bears of North America are called grizzly bears. The name comes from the white tips to their brown hairs, which make them look old and grey. Grizzled comes from the French word *gris*, which means grey.

Grizzly bear

Angry bear!

An angry bear makes itself look big and frightening! It rears up on its back legs and shows off its sharp teeth and claws.

Are bears clever?

Bears are very intelligent animals. They have large brains, are very curious and are good at finding their way around. American black bears are thought to be the most intelligent of all the bears.

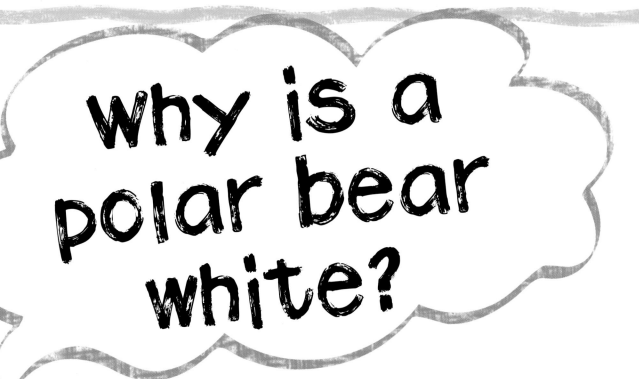

Why is a polar bear white?

A polar bear is the same colour as the snow and ice where it lives. This helps it to hide from its prey, because it is hard to see against the white background. The hairs in its coat are not really white. They are hollow tubes, which look white when they reflect the light.

Polar bear

Ghost bear

what are ghost bears?

Some American black bears are born with a white coat, which makes them look like ghosts. These white ghost bears live only on a few islands in western Canada.

star bear!

Ancient Greeks believed that the Great Bear star pattern was placed in the sky by their chief god, Zeus.

which bear is famous?

The giant panda is famous as the symbol of the World Wide Fund for Nature (WWF). This rare bear was chosen partly because of its black-and-white fur. The symbol could be photocopied in black and white, without the need for any colours.

Write

Think up a story about a ghost bear that lives in a zoo!

27

Why are moon bears naughty?

Moon bear

Moon bears often visit farmers' fields and steal their crops, such as maize (sweetcorn). The bears use their sharp teeth to tear the maize cobs off the stalks. Farmers often hunt or trap the bears to save their crops.

can people get close to bears?

Yes! Tourists can get close to polar bears near the town of Churchill in Canada. They travel in big, strong buses, which keep them safe from the powerful, curious bears.

Polar bear

Panda peril!

Giant pandas have lost their homes because people have cut down the forests where they live. However, people are working hard to protect and save these bears.

Draw

Design a poster to show why we need to look after bears and how we can help them.

why do bears eat rubbish?

People's rubbish contains lots of left-over food for bears to eat. A bear can smell the rubbish from a long way away and will return to it over and over again. When bears spend a lot of time near people, they lose their fear of humans and can become dangerous.

Quiz time

Do you remember what you have read about bears? Here are some questions to test your memory. The pictures will help you. If you get stuck, read the pages again.

3. Do pandas ever stop eating?

page 12

4. Which bear has the longest tongue?

page 13

1. Which bear is not a bear?

page 7

5. Are sloth bears noisy?

page 14

2. Are bears good at climbing trees?

page 10

6. Do bears have picnics?

page 17

7. Which bear gives birth in a snow cave?

page 19

11. Which bear is grizzly?

page 25

8. Why do bears feast in autumn?

page 19

12. Why is a polar bear white?

page 26

9. How big are bear cubs?

page 21

13. Why do bears eat rubbish?

page 29

10. Do bears give piggybacks?

page 22

Answers

1. A koala
2. Yes, bears can scramble up tree trunks easily
3. Not very often
4. The sun bear
5. Yes – when they feed at a termite mound, the noise can be heard 100 metres away
6. Teddy bears might do, but real bears don't
7. The polar bear
8. Because there is lots of food for them to eat
9. They are only very small
10. Sloth bear mothers give the cubs piggybacks
11. The brown bear of North America, called the grizzly bear
12. It can't be seen against the snow and ice, so it can hide from its prey
13. Rubbish contains lots of left-over food for them to eat

Index